C-130 Hercules in the RAF

CLIVE BENNETT

AMBERLEY

Dedicated to Ronald and Joyce Bennett

First published 2018

Amberley Publishing
The Hill, Stroud,
Gloucestershire, GL5 4EP

www.amberley-books.com

ISBN 978 1 4456 5207 8 (print)
ISBN 978 1 4456 5208 5 (ebook)

British Library Cataloguing in Publication Data.
A catalogue record for this book is available from the British Library.

Typeset in 11pt on 14pt Celeste.
Origination by Amberley Publishing.
Printed in the UK.

Contents

Chapter One

From its introduction in the mid-1960s, when the first aircraft were delivered, through the various humanitarian missions, the Falkland Islands conflict, operations in Iraq and Afghanistan, right up to the introduction of the J version,

XV176, the first of the fleet, during assembly at Marietta. (Lockheed Martin)

RAF Hercules on the assembly line in the 1960s. (Lockheed Martin)

this book will cover all key aspects of the C-130's remarkable history and military service with the Royal Air Force. The Lockheed C-130 Hercules – or as some call them, the 'Fat Albert' – has completed over fifty years' service for the Royal Air Force and this book is a tribute to the sterling operational career of this truly iconic aircraft and the men and women who have served on them.

Whenever the Royal Air Force has a need for an aircraft to deliver humanitarian aid, or deploy troops to a particular hotspot around the world, to ensure supplies are received or to support a war fighting army, the Hercules has performed like no other aircraft since the Douglas Dakota of Second World War fame. Designed with an internal hold dimension of 40 feet in length, 9 feet 11 inches width and a 9-foot height, the same size and dimensions of the American railroad boxcar, the Hercules could carry a wide variety of cargo over distances of up to 2,950 miles, at a height of 33,000 feet. With a cruising speed of 290 knots, True Air Speed (TAS) for the K version and 320 (TAS) for the J version, they offered a great improvement over the eclectic mix of predecessors, the Blackburn Beverley, Handley Page Hastings and Armstrong Whitworth Argosy, all of which continued in support, albeit in a secondary role, within RAF Transport Command once the Hercules was introduced to service. This gave an advanced leap in transport capabilities that the RAF never had at its disposal until the Hercules joined the active inventory.

The Hercules has proved to be a great success in the hands of the Royal Air Force; this was further endorsed by the fact that they were the launch customer for the updated and greatly improved J model in the early 2000s. With over five decades of operations under its belt, the Hercules continues to give outstanding service with the RAF, and with an expected retirement date of 2030, this would total a service career of a staggering sixty-four years of continuous operations. Even with the arrival of the new Airbus A400M Atlas into the RAF inventory, the Hercules' career is going to be some task for the new Atlas to eclipse!

Rolling out a completed aircraft at Lockheed's Marietta plant in the 1960s. (Lockheed Martin)

When the British-designed HS-681 short take-off jet transport project was cancelled by Prime Minister Harold Wilson, he announced that the replacement would be the Lockheed C-130 Hercules. Wilson gave two reasons why this decision had been made: its availability and its lower cost per unit. The latter would save the British taxpayer two thirds of the predicted $560 million costs, against the HS-681.

A total of sixty-six airframes were ordered, which carried serials XV176 – XV223 and XV290 – XV307, with the first scheduled for delivery during 1966, and the Lockheed manufacturing plant in Marietta, Georgia, geared up to deliver four aircraft a month beginning in March 1967. Renamed the Hercules C.Mk 1, the first aircraft was handed over to the RAF on 16 December 1966.

A ceremony was held at Marietta, where the first aircraft (XV177) was handed over to the RAF. XV177 left the Lockheed facility on Saturday 17 December 1967 for Marshall Aerospace, located at Cambridge Airport, arriving on Monday 19th. Marshall's first interaction with the RAF Hercules was to install the UK-specified equipment when they arrived in England, as well as to transform them from natural metal into light brown and sand camouflage. Once XV177 was attired in its new uniform and equipment, she was flown to Boscombe Down to begin trials.

One of the differences between the British aircraft and the C-130H Hercules was the UK-manufactured equipment carried aboard RAF versions, with over 80 per cent of radio, navigational, interphone and autopilot installation being sourced from UK-based suppliers and installed by Marshall.

This version became the C-130K, designated as such by Lockheed to differentiate the specification differences of the UK variant from other models within their product portfolio.

Even though the 'K' variant had most of the operating systems of the C-130H, it did have a few peculiarities. For example, it did not have the Auxiliary Power Unit (APU) as fitted to the 'H' model. It did, however, have the same H-15 engines. The main difference with the RAF aircraft was the cargo floor, which was altered to UK guidance and included a roller system so that British pallets and airdrop systems could be installed. This made RAF Hercules non-standard and incompatible with other Hercules operators. The fleet were modified by enabling fitting adaptors that alleviated this problem, though after the incompatibility had caused issues on NATO operations.

The first aircraft manufactured for the RAF (XV176) was retained by Lockheed for six months, conducting flight trials and tests. It was finally delivered to the RAF during the middle of 1967, and the remainder of the fleet were all delivered by the end of 1969.

RAF Thorney Island (West Sussex) saw the first phase of operational flying, Operational Conversion Unit (OCU) 242 Squadron being established from 7 April 1967, the date of the first aircraft delivery. August 1967 saw the Hercules operating for the first time from RAF Lyneham, Wiltshire.

Chapter Two

With the Operational Conversion Unit up and running, and as more aircrews became cleared for type, the Hercules started to venture to other RAF bases around the world. The first squadron to start operating the aircraft was 36 Squadron, who started operations in August 1967; 36 Squadron was based at RAF Colerne, flying the Handley Page Hastings, and the change of equipment to the Hercules also signalled a relocation to RAF Lyneham. This was followed quite rapidly by 48 Squadron, who became operational during October 1967, just prior to being deployed overseas to RAF Changi, Singapore, as part of Transport Command Far East, returning in 1971 to Lyneham. 48 Squadron's activities in the Far East consisted of various operations and exercises; some of these operations came under the control and responsibility of SEATO (South East Asia Treaty Organisation). One particular mission involved operating to Saigon to resupply the embassy, as well as to transport the occasional passenger into or out of the country. These flights were somewhat interesting as the war was still raging and the specified approach procedure into and out of Saigon Airport and the intense radio traffic with the distress frequencies active certainly focused the crew's attention while partaking in such operations!

During 1968 Lyneham started to receive aircraft to equip 24 Squadron; again, this involved transferring operations from RAF Colerne to Lyneham. 24 Squadron has operated the Hercules (all varieties) in RAF service continuously up to the present day; currently this impressive record stands at a grand total of forty-nine years.

RAF Fairford in Gloucestershire became the next base to welcome the Hercules when both 30 Squadron and 47 Squadron moved in to take up operations, in June and February 1968 respectively. These two squadrons remained at Fairford until they were also transferred to RAF Lyneham during 1971. The last squadron that initially operated the Hercules was 70 Squadron, which started operating the aircraft from Cyprus during 1970, remaining on the island until they also transferred back to the UK and RAF Lyneham during 1975.

XV196 undergoing front-line maintenance while on charge with 48 Squadron. (B. Ragg)

XV179 just prior to carrying out another sortie while serving with 48 Squadron at RAF Changi. (B. Ragg)

XV194 of 48 Squadron in the dispersal at RAF Changi. (B. Ragg)

XV307 of 48 Squadron in June 1970, on the crushed coral temporary airstrip at Mahé in the Seychelles after offloading a piston for the engine of an RFA ship. (B. Ragg)

One of the aircraft's first missions was to assist the withdrawal of British forces from Aden in 1967, when the country became an independent Marxist republic in May of that year. A series of shuttle flights were instigated using Hercules as well as Britannias and Belfasts between Aden and RAF Muharraq on Bahrain Island, starting in earnest during August through to October, then finally during the period 5–30 November, when all aircraft types within RAF Air Support Command were active in transporting 6,000 troops and 400 tons of equipment out of RAF Khormaksar, Aden.

The Hercules C.Mk 1 was powered by four Allison T-56A-15 turboprop engines delivering 4,200 shp from each, mated to a Hamilton Standard 54H60 four-bladed propeller. The basic weight was 78,000 lb approx., with a maximum take-off weight of 155,000 lb fully laden. The aircraft could carry 63,000 lb of fuel and cover a distance of 2,950 nautical miles with a 3,000 lb payload on board.

The C.Mk 1 version of the Hercules was also capable of carrying ninety-two passengers, or sixty-two paratroopers, seventy-four stretcher patients, six pallets of goods or one Gazelle helicopter within its hold. This capability ensured that the aircraft was in high demand for the United Kingdom's military services, but it quickly became apparent that more capability was required to meet the ongoing requirements for the Hercules force to get the most out of the aircraft.

Chapter Three

With so many squadrons operating the Hercules, the Lyneham Transport Wing (LTW) was formed during 1970; this had the advantage of having a shared pool of aircraft, maintenance, equipment, spares and all flight training functions, all at the same location.

XV200, in original dark and light brown camouflage with white cockpit roof, landing at Brize Norton during April 1977. (Mick Freer)

Above: XV219 at RAF Lyneham in August 1975. (Mick Freer)

Right: Brand new C-130s on the ramp at RAF Thorney Island during the late 1960s. (Dedicated to the K Crews Collection)

Once the LTW was fully operational and functioning within the RAF, its aircraft were utilised on many transportation missions, including supporting other RAF squadrons whenever they were deployed away from their home base, transporting all that is needed to keep a fully functioning squadron operational by getting everything from spare parts to personnel to their destination on time and complete. As well as supporting the RAF, the Hercules has assisted in the deployment of Army assets throughout many operational requirements, and has also acted as a platform in getting airborne troops into the right place at the right time!

The Hercules was operated by the standard transport crew of the time then in RAF service, comprising a pilot, co-pilot, navigator, flight engineer and air loadmaster. All training on the aircraft was carried out at squadron level with the Operational Conversion Squadron (OCU), No. 242, continuing in the training role for all flight crew, with all the flight crew graduating together.

With RAF Lyneham having six squadrons of the C-130K and operating on the pool principle, none of the aircraft carried individual squadron markings, although there were a number of airframes that carried the markings of all squadrons that were flying from the base, as well as a few that carried the Lyneham station crest proudly on the fuselage. All the aircraft were individually identified on the airframes with the aircraft's serial number, which was carried either side of the radome, on the fuselage side behind the RAF roundel and on the tail.

XV212 sat on the ramp at Thorney Island in brilliant sunshine. (Dedicated to the K Crews Collection)

XV194 and XV181
high above the clouds
on a training mission.
(Dedicated to the
K Crews Collection)

Above left: XV182 on a supply-dropping training mission. (Dedicated to the K Crews Collection)

Above right: XV307 being loaded with supplies for a relief flight while the crew discuss their upcoming mission and drop zone target. (Dedicated to the K Crews Collection)

While the Hercules is known for its capability to assist with military deployments, its other main role is that of humanitarian support; regularly during its career it has been called upon to respond to emergencies, assisting the United Nations in such missions around the globe. One emergency that the RAF reacted to was to support the Red Cross in Jordan following the devastating earthquake that shook that country in 1970. This was quite rapidly followed by support in East Pakistan (Bangladesh) after a disastrous cyclone hit the country and the RAF flew into Calcutta under the auspices of Operation Burlap with medical supplies to try to aid in stopping or stemming the outbreak of cholera.

XV186 and XV187 being prepared at RAF Lyneham prior to operating relief flights in Africa. (Dedicated to the K Crews Collection)

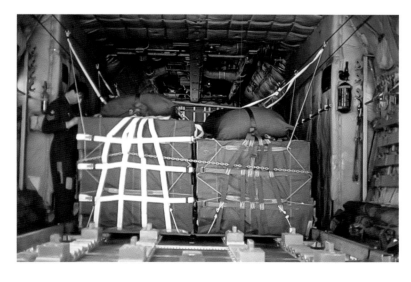

1-ton container in a 48 Squadron Hercules, ready for a training drop. (B. Ragg)

Above: XV205, sat on the ramp at the former Salisbury Airport, Rhodesia, while operating relief flights. The airport is still active but under its new name of Harare, Zimbabwe. (Dedicated to the K Crew Collection)

Right: A three-ship formation of C-130Ks poses for the camera while flying over a patchwork of fields in southern England. (Dedicated to the K Crews Collection)

During 1972 the Lyneham Hercules fleet was called into service once again, flying relief flights to the Philippines after a typhoon caused torrential flooding, and on Christmas Day they also started flying into Nicaragua on relief operations after an earthquake caused widespread damage, food shortages and disease for the estimated 1 million inhabitants of Managua, the country's capital.

1973 brought yet more demand for Lyneham's Hercules and personnel; four aircraft were dispatched to Nepal to perform airdrops of food and supplies to the starving inhabitants, something that they excelled in. This operation (Khana Cascade) resulted in 1,964 tons of cargo being delivered over a twenty-nine-day period into a relatively inaccessible mountain region in the west of the country. This task was particularly significant, being the largest since the Berlin Airlift, and was on par with deliveries of rice, maize and grain to the local inhabitants. The aircraft flew out to the region via RAF Akrotiri and Masirah and on to Bhairawa, close to the Nepalese border. The operation lasted from February 1973 until the last flight on 30 March 1973.

1974 was a relatively quiet year, except that a coup in Cyprus by Turkey forced the withdrawal of service personnel and civilians from Kingsfield, Dhekalia, firstly to RAF Akrotiri and then onto Britain; overall some 5,148 different nationals from forty-six countries were airlifted out during this operation.

An unidentified C-130K conducting low-level operations along the coast. This type of flying affords the aircraft and crew a good training environment. (Chaz Gelder)

XV176, the first of the fleet for the RAF.
(C. Bennett)

The end of the Vietnam War also brought a need for RAF Hercules to be called into operation to evacuate the British staff from the embassy in Saigon during 1975. Aircraft were subjected to mortar fire while at the main airport; luckily, though, none received any damage and all flew out unscathed.

A similar evacuation was necessary four years later when the Shah of Iran was toppled from power in 1979, with Western nationals having to leave the country quickly from Tehran Airport, once again in the safe hands of the RAF Hercules. In 1984 and 1985 the drought conditions in Ethiopia brought a natural disaster to areas of the African country. The RAF Hercules were quickly called into service supporting humanitarian relief flights, operating out of Addis Ababa Airport under the remit of Operation Bushel. Responsible for delivering almost 31,500 tons of food to stricken communities throughout the country, the operation lasted until November of 1985, over 40 per cent of all deliveries being airdropped from the aircraft.

1992 saw the need for the Hercules to support UNHCR (United Nations High Commissioner for Refugees) operations within the former Yugoslavia. Deployed to Zagreb Airport, they started operating relief flights into Sarajevo under Operation Cheshire, moving to Ancona on Italy's Adriatic coast because of the danger to crews who were stationed at Zagreb. These flights were also suspended for a period of time between April and September 1995 because it was deemed too

C-130K XV206,
a Special Forces
aircraft, sits
in one of the
many hangars
at Lyneham.
(C. Bennett)

XV223 under
threatening skies
at RAF Lyneham
during 1998.
(C. Bennett)

Transiting to the
Low Fly Area in
Wales (LFA 7),
XV221 is captured
above the Welsh
border during
1999. (C. Bennett)

dangerous to fly into and out of Sarajevo. The Hercules airlifted supplies into the city and injured children back to RAF Lyneham to receive medical treatment, with over 1,916 such sorties being flown. These operations came to an end on 9 January 1996 following the signing of the Bosnian peace agreement in Dayton, Ohio, USA. RAF support was also key in Operation Resolute, which began in 1995 to move personnel and equipment into Split, Sarajevo and Tuzla, with Hercules moving a contingent of 13,000 British peacekeeping troops into the Balkans. Continued operations in support of Operation Agricola in 1999, in response to the Kosovo crisis, saw eight Hercules aircraft deploying to RAF Bruggen in Germany, Lyneham engineering personnel and movements staff positioning to Thessaloniki in Greece and Skopje in Macedonia respectively. Transporting troops initially required C-130s to fly eighty-four missions within the first four days; in all some 460 flights were flown supporting KFOR operations within the Balkans, delivering more than 4,400 troops and 276 vehicles by the end of operation on 16 July.

Maintenance crews working on a C-130K engine on the flight line at RAF Lyneham. (C. Bennett)

Close-up silhouette of a C-130K during an air-to-air sortie in the late 1990s. (C. Bennett)

XV214 at medium altitude over the English countryside on a typical autumnal day. (Chaz Gelder)

One of the main tasks for the Hercules fleet was the delivery of men and materials by airdrop; this enabled supplies to be dispatched into areas where it was not possible to land the aircraft. The size of airdrop loads varied, with the RAF using the following methods of delivery for the respective loads: MSP (Medium Stressed Platform), HSP (Heavy Stressed Platform) and ULLA (Ultra Low

Operational patch for the relief operations in Ethiopia. (Todd Shugart)

Level Airdrop) and Harness Pack (HP), all of which were designed to best fit the styles and make-up of the load being despatched on any given operation or training flight. Many different operational exercises were undertaken to help to hone the skills of the crews in carrying out airdrops, with exercises like Bold Guard and Deep Furrow taking place at regular intervals. Bold Guard was a recurring exercise, with the first taking place during 1974 and continuing until 1986. Held within the military designated area of Denmark and northern Germany, primarily around the Baltic Sea, this was a major NATO training exercise which involved troops and equipment from the UK, USA, Denmark and Germany. The first year saw one particular part of the exercise which involved the insertion of 600 British airborne troops, who were airdropped on the night of 11 September; this task utilised thirty-six C-130Ks, over half of the RAF's active fleet then in service.

Exercise Deep Furrow was a yearly event that first occurred during the 1960s. Held in Turkey, this was a dual parachute and marine training operation and once again the C-130Ks played a major role in the insertion of parachute troops.

The local area around RAF Lyneham was always heavily utilised, with Hercules in the circuit nearly every day; the sight and sound of the aircraft undergoing hours of touch and goes at the hands of a newly commissioned or a fully qualified pilot keeping his or her hours active was a common sight, day or night. The Hercules had a long association with the Wiltshire base, but this all came to an end on 27 June 2011, when the last aircraft took to the air for the final time when the Hercules force moved lock, stock and barrel to RAF Brize Norton in Oxfordshire.

XV305, sat on the ramp at RAF Lyneham with 70 Squadron markings on the tail and the 1916–2010 anniversary of the squadron commemorated on the fuselage. (Ian Harding)

XV301, a C.Mk 3, during a visit to the Salisbury Plain Training Area (SPTA) at Deptford Down. (Ian Harding)

A C-130K traversing Low Fly Area LFA 7 at Corris on the Mach Loop. (Ian Harding)

XV188, a Special Forces capable C-130K, on a training mission through Wales. (K. Wills)

XV210, a grey and green C-130K, visiting RAF Fairford during the annual Air Tattoo in 1996. (C. Bennett)

Left: Another load being prepared for transport to the former Yugoslavia aboard C-130K C3 XV303. (C. Bennett)

Below: XV206 on display during the RAF Forces open day during 1998. (C. Bennett)

Chapter Four

Even though the Hercules was in great demand during the 1970s, one airframe was withdrawn from the fleet and added to the Meteorological Research Flight (MRF) at RAE Farnborough. Serial XV208 was selected for conversion and was reallocated the design specification of a Lockheed C-130K W2 variant. She had been delivered to the RAF on 22 September 1967 and was part of 48 Squadron, based at RAF Changi, Singapore. Taking over the role from Vickers Varsity WF425, the airframe was extensively modified to fit its new task; the weather radar was moved to the top of the fuselage to allow the long 22-foot nose probe to be installed on the front of the airframe below the cockpit windows and she also had underwing fuel tanks, similar to those fitted to C-130As, added to extend her range.

XV208 *Snoopy* gets airborne from RAF Brize Norton in June 1984. (Stuart Freer – Touchdown Aviation)

Above: XV208 *Snoopy*
seen while airborne over
the English countryside.
(Dedicated to the K Crews
Collection)

Left: Meteorological Research
Flight patch showing
Snoopy flying through
various weather conditions.
(Todd Shugart)

Modified by Marshall at Cambridge during 1972, the aircraft was fitted out and able to take up its new role. The advantage that *Snoopy* gave to the MRF over previous airframes flown by the flight was immense: it could comfortably cruise at much higher speeds and altitudes (25,000 feet) than was previously possible, as well as being able to carry vastly more equipment. Operations were carried out all over the globe; from the dry temperatures of the desert through to the monsoons of Asia, flying over 1,800 research sorties during its career, *Snoopy* has been there monitoring and analysing the weather and gathering important data. As an Airborne Laboratory, the aircraft was crewed by RAF personnel, with Met Office technical staff; the Ministry of Defence still owned and funded the aircraft but the Met Office payed for its own staff and all equipment carried, which had an estimated cost in the region of £800,000 per year. Numerous international research projects were also undertaken; the payments for operations were all in Swiss francs and during the early 1990s a severe fall in the value of the pound against foreign currencies put the Met Office overdrawn on its budget, which put the aircraft's future in severe doubt going forward. *Snoopy* was under review and the RAF did indeed make a statement saying that the aircraft was at risk, as all defence related projects were when there was a requirement to try and balance the books.

XV208 *Snoopy* prior to relocating back to the RAE after servicing at Marshall Aerospace. (Marshall)

XV208 receiving her TP400-D6 engine on the inner port pylon. (Marshall)

With the new engine fitted for the Airbus A400M, XV208 is readied for flight. (Marshall)

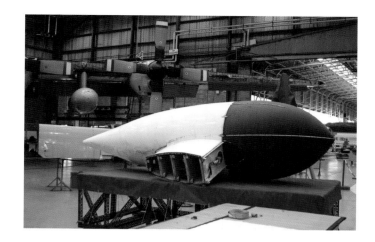

During conversion back to a conventional aircraft, the radar housing that used to be mounted above the cockpit on XV208 sits in the hangar at Marshall. (Marshall)

One of the most important missions that Snoopy undertook was just after the first Gulf War, when the retreating Iraqi Army left Kuwait and decided to set fire to the many oil fields in the area. Snoopy flew through the blackened smoke as it rose up into the atmosphere, analysing and monitoring the pollution and assisting to help predict any health issues; she was one of the first aircraft on site and an extremely valuable asset.

With its snout, the aircraft has the ability to improve the art of weather forecasting; linked to a series of computers, she could monitor climate change as well as keeping a close eye on the ozone layer and reviewing the hole size and reporting on the effects of global warming, while also looking at man-made pollutants like sulphur dioxide and other greenhouse gases.

Snoopy relocated to Boscombe Down in March 1994, as did various other airframes from the Defence Evaluation and Research Agency (DERA), which all moved en masse when RAE Farnborough finally closed during 1998. Once there, she settled into operating alongside the Empire Test Pilots School (EPTS), a long-term resident of the airfield. She was flying on average two to three times per week, which equates to approximately 500 hours per year, booked up well in advance by research teams to carry out missions and operations globally.

On 21 March 2001 *Snoopy*'s flying days with the MRF came to an end as the flight was disbanded, the RAF's duties being taken over by the National Environmental Research Council (NERC) who, in conjunction with the Facility for Airborne Atmospheric Measurement (FAAM), took over operations, although on a smaller scale. This wasn't, though, the end of her flying career. She was ferried back to Marshall at Cambridge and modified once again, this time appearing more like a conventional Hercules; the main change was putting her radar back in her nose and removing the long striped snout. The other main change was the installation of a TP400-D6 engine on the port inner engine position for a series of tests for the A400 Atlas series of aircraft.

A total of eighteen trial flights were undertaken with the aircraft in this configuration, totalling fifty-four hours; its final flight occurred on 30 September 2009. She stayed at Marshall's facility until April 2015, slowly giving up many parts as a donor aircraft, which she did for an additional five years after she last graced the skies.

The end came in a somewhat undignified manner when she was finally taken apart on site, although her pilot's yoke was handed over to Daz James, the last pilot to fly *Snoopy* and take her into the air. There was a somewhat happy end for *Snoopy*'s characteristic nose probe when a section of it was preserved at the Met Office headquarters in Exeter, along with a panel detailing her role with the Metrological Flight, all of which are still on display there to this day.

XV208 in her new guise of test aircraft, with the new power plant undergoing ground testing. (Marshall)

A sad end: her flying days over, XV208 has her front fuselage severed from the rest of the airframe prior to final cutting up. Note the red nose. (Marshall)

Chapter Five

Since the Hercules' introduction into service with the RAF, its association with Marshall Aerospace has been established and the company have been fulfilling all the heavy maintenance and modifications work required for the whole fleet while in RAF service. Marshall have also become the main service centre for Hercules operators throughout Europe and for some Middle East operators. RAF aircraft have been subjected to many modifications over the years, beginning in 1978 when thirty airframes were selected for extensions to their fuselages, increasing the length by 15 feet; these comprised two plugs, one behind the flight deck and cockpit area, while the other was fitted just forward of the rear cargo ramp area.

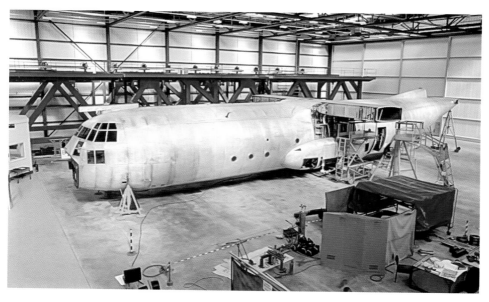

An unidentified C-130K undergoing fuselage fatigue testing in Hangar 21. (Marshall)

XV189 and XV217 undergoing conversion to C.Mk 3 during 1980 by having the two additional 15-foot plugs inserted into their fuselages. (Marshall)

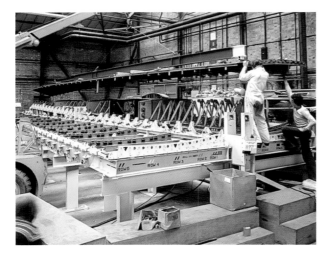

Centre wing refurbishment being carried out during the late 1970s. (Marshall)

XV294's front end, with the new plug attached, sits behind the Stretch Team, 1980. (Marshall)

XV305, the first C-130 undergoing centre wing section change, on 7 May 1975 with various Marshall Aerospace and RAF personnel inspecting the work. (Marshall)

XV299, the last stretched C3 variant to be converted, during its handover back to the RAF during November 1985. (Marshall)

The designation for these aircraft was changed and they became C.Mk 3, which gave a 27 per cent increase in load carrying capability over the C.Mk 1. This actually equates to the possible addition of a further twenty-six paratroopers, eight additional pallets or one additional vehicle per aircraft. XV223 was ferried back to Lockheed's facility at Marietta, Georgia, to be the first aircraft to undergo this modification. All the plug sections were then manufactured by Lockheed and transported over to Marshall for installation on the remainder of the twenty-nine aircraft to be upgraded; this work was completed during the mid-1980s.

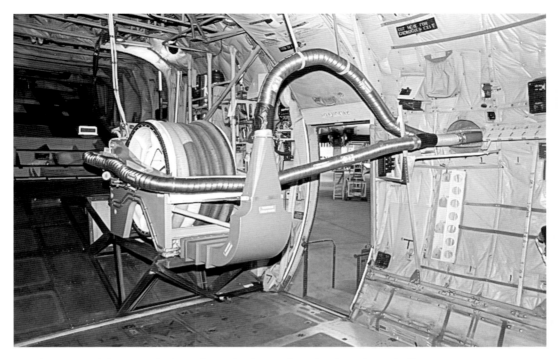

Another view of the HDU, looking from the front of the fuselage. (Marshall)

XV296 while undergoing trials with its hose deployed. (Marshall)

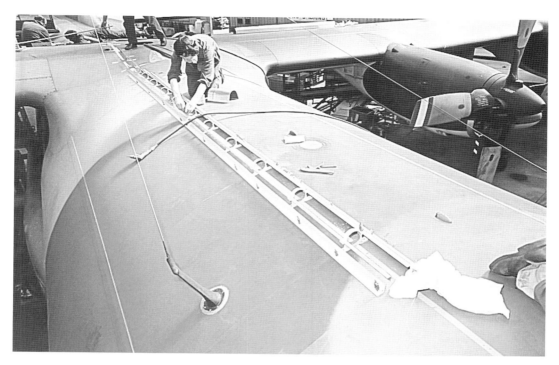

A C-130K having its in-flight refuelling probe fitted prior to operations in the Falklands Conflict, 1982. (Marshall)

XV218 test-flying the new probe during 1982. (Marshall)

During 1979 the entire fleet of Hercules had to undergo the fitting of a redesigned wing centre section following the failure of a specimen section that was undergoing fatigue testing by Lockheed Martin. All current aircraft were subjected to the modification, which was completed by the end of the year. Another modification that the fleet undertook during the time period 1979–85 came under the Fatigue Life Extension Programme and was applied once again to the Hercules outer wing sections; this work consisted of the wing joints and engine mounts being modified to give the required extension to flying life.

The Falklands Conflict of 1982 brought an urgent modification to the entire fleet of Hercules. Marshall completed the installation of an in-flight refuelling probe on top of the cockpit area position; XV200 was first to be modified and was delivered back to the RAF at Lyneham a mere twenty-one days after arriving at Marshall for the modifications to be carried out. This helped to support the deployment and capability of the transport fleet in getting supplies and stores in theatre while incurring the least inconvenience. After hostilities ceased, it was decided to fit all the remaining aircraft with the in-flight refuelling probes to increase the capability for the whole Hercules fleet.

Six Hercules C.Mk 1 aircraft were converted for the tanker role and designated C.1 (K), the first aircraft being delivered to RAF Lyneham on 5 July 1982 and the sixth and final example following three weeks later. This operation later transferred to the VC10 force and all the Hercules were converted back to a pure transportation role; the tanker operation did last much longer than was originally intended, though. The first aircraft that was converted back (XV192) was followed by the remaining five (XV201, 203, 204, 213 and XV296), all of which finally ended up back at the Marshall facility in storage; two of these were later refurbished and sold to the Sri Lankan Air Force.

XV192 and XV187 in formation, with 192 trailing a hose. (Marshall)

C-130 pilot's eye view of
the refuelling process
from a C-130 tanker.
(Dedicated to the K Crews
Collection)

XV200 receives a
top up from XV296.
(Dedicated to the K Crews
Collection)

The fit for the tanker aircraft consisted of a standard Flight Refuelling Limited Hose Drum Unit (HDU) Mark 17B that was located on the back of the loading ramp, the drogue box being located on the cargo door itself; this enabled the aircraft to remain fully pressurised while in flight to the rendezvous point (RP). Once on station the Hercules had to de-pressurise to give fuel, the crews having to go onto oxygen until the transfer was complete and the aircraft could be pressurised again. Tanker aircraft made use of surplus Andover fuel tanks that were carried in the main hold/cabin of the aircraft. This increased the total fuel carried on these aircraft to 28,800 lb. Trials began on 8 June 1982 and these initially consisted of just deploying the drogue; the aircraft then moved to Boscombe Down on 11 June to begin trials with a Harrier, a set of tests involving only 'dry contacts' to understand the effects on the receiving aircraft. Some issues ensued for the Harrier, with the drogue unit causing airflow problems, so the Hercules was moved back to Marshall for more tests to gain better experience of the effect of the drogue unit when deployed.

Successful wet contacts were undertaken on 21 June, with the Hercules once again deploying to Boscombe Down and the A&AEE, and following a vast array of testing with the frontline aircraft then in service with the RAF (Buccaneer, Nimrod, Phantom and Hercules) and a Sea Harrier from the Navy, all made effective refuellings at various heights and distances.

The overall time period from conception to active introduction of the Hercules C.Mk 1 (K) variant was a mere eighty-seven days for completion of four aircraft from design to fully operational, a truly magnificent feat of engineering that included design, manufacture, installation and ground and flight testing.

Marshall had more modification work to add to their portfolio when in 1989 some aircraft were subjected to new integral wing tanks; this followed corrosion being

XV296 in flight prior to conducting dry contact trials. (Marshall)

Above: A C-130K tanker with its hose deployed. Note the lights, which tell the receiver when fuel is flowing. (Marshall)

Right: Plugged in and fuel flowing: a C-130K getting topped up. (Dedicated to the K Crews Collection)

found, the cause being a batch of contaminated fuel. Post-1991, all aircraft were fitted with a new navigational equipment suite and Global Positioning System (GPS).

Another trial that Marshall were heavily involved in was the installation of the new power plant for the upcoming C-130J. In 1994 C-130K XV181 was selected to trial the new engine and six-bladed propeller for the new aircraft design to gather data for Lockheed Martin and the other members of the UK C-130J industrial support group, all of which had a vested interest in the forthcoming variant.

Since 1966 Marshall have been carrying out all major servicing on the RAF Hercules, with a frequency of every six years (C-130K) and ten years (C-130J)

Left: C-130J engine test aircraft XV181 while undergoing trials at Marshall during 1994. (Marshall)

Below: ZH878, a C-130J, during engine run ups at Cambridge. (Marshall)

through the facility. A corrosion control process was started during 1976 to strip, protect and repaint the fleet; this was finished during 1979 and had become a normal procedure every ten years or so since inception.

Marshall were also fundamental when the C.1 and C.3 versions were withdrawn from service; the majority of the fleet were returned to the Cambridgeshire airfield for decommissioning, with some airframes being ferried back to Lockheed in Georgia in a part-exchange agreement, with new Hercules C-130J aircraft moving the other way to start their service life with the RAF, who were the launch customer for the new variant.

Chapter Six

When Argentina invaded the Falkland Islands in April 1982, the British Government assembled and sent a task force (TF 317) down to the South Atlantic to liberate the islanders and islands, bringing the land back into British hands. Because of the distances involved, the RAF was tasked with establishing an air supply route down to the nearest airfield to the Falklands (Wideawake, Ascension Island) from the UK, a distance of approximately 4,000 miles. RAF Hercules were at the forefront on this supply route, which routed from Lyneham to Dakar (Senegal) and sometimes Gibraltar, depending on the weather and the strength of the headwinds. The squadrons involved were Nos 24, 30, 47 and 70, all of which had access to fifty aircraft from the LTW, fourteen of the larger C.Mk 3 and thirty-six of the standard C.Mk 1 variants being utilised. Although all of the active squadrons based at Lyneham took part in the air supply, Nos 24 and 30 were only cleared to carry provisions for the task force down to Wideawake; 47 and 70 Squadrons were trained and cleared for the tactical operations, including air drops where applicable.

Tanker XV201 sat on the apron at Marshall Aerospace after conversion for its new role, showing off its new drogue. (Marshall)

Receiver's eye view as the probe is guided toward the drogue during refuelling, C-130 to C-130. (Marshall)

XV204 sitting on the apron at Mount Pleasant Airfield, Port Stanley. (Dedicated to the K Crews Collection)

An unidentified C-130K viewed over
Port Stanley after the Falklands Conflict
was complete. (Marshall)

The first operational flight in theatre happened on 3 April; a Hercules carrying
a team from the Mobile Air Movements Squadron took off to establish an Air
Head for all Hercules flights from the UK, which totalled over 150 in the first three
weeks – a far greater number than first expected.

As more flights were dispatched from the UK, Hercules were leaving Lyneham
on average every four hours, delivering over 1,340 tons of supplies onto Wideawake
Airfield.

One of the most important concerns around the Hercules and the new supply
route down to the South Atlantic was the aircraft's range. Its current maximum
range capability was 2,300 miles, which meant that fuel stops had to be made en
route. Lyneham's engineering unit did come up with an idea to increase the range
by fitting two auxiliary fuel tanks in the forward hold area of the Hercules. These
tanks increased the range by approximately 1,000 miles by adding 1,650 imperial
gallons of fuel; a further modification to increase the amount of fuel carried
by fitting four fuel tanks was carried out on a single aircraft. This aircraft was
re-designated Hercules LR4 for the duration of the trial and although it did have
to give away a reduced payload (maximum of 10,000 lb), it was put to good use as
because of its reduced carrying capacity it was ideal for dropping supplies to the
task force as they approached the Falkland Islands.

The need to make some aircraft capable of receiving fuel while airborne was
the only viable option open to the RAF at the time; this would negate the need for
them to land during flights into and out of theatre, which would also save on transit
times. The addition of the capability to receive airborne refuelling greatly aided
the Hercules in delivering all the supplies in theatre, crews gaining experiencing in
this difficult operation after many hours of training in this demanding role.

An RAF Tristar from 216 Squadron refuelling a C-130K. (Marshall)

The inside view of a C-130 tanker, showing the four additional tanks within the fuselage. (Marshall)

Above left: C-130 tanker HDU trials aircraft at Marshall Aerospace in 1982. (Marshall)

Above right: The official patch for 1312 Flight. (Todd Shugart)

With airborne refuelling on the Hercules, a world record was recorded on 18 June 1982 when Flt Lt Locke and his crew flew XV179 and, refuelling from an RAF Victor aircraft, managed to stay aloft for twenty-eight hours and three minutes to drop supplies on Mount Kent, the normal time of twenty-four hours and five minutes being increased by headwinds on both the southbound and homeward legs.

Once hostilities had ceased, it became clear that the RAF would have to deploy a force of aircraft permanently in the area, so there was a need for tanker aircraft to become part of the permanent detachment of aircraft that were stationed at Mount Pleasant Airfield as part of the defence of the Falkland Islands. The complex was active from 1985 and 1312 Flight was established with C.Mk 1 (K) aircraft to provide airborne refuelling to the RAF's detachment of four Phantoms (later Tornado F3s) of 1435 Flight, also stationed at the airfield. The Phantoms' primary objectives were the airborne defence of the region, flying top cover and keeping the no-fly zones free from potentially hostile aircraft. This operation came to an end for the Hercules during 1996 when the operation transferred to 101 Squadron and the VC10s from Brize Norton, one aircraft being deployed on a rotational basis. The RAF did have a Hercules deployed on the Falkland Islands at Mount Pleasant Airfield for maritime reconnaissance missions, search and rescue (SAR) operations and for air supply drops to the Army on the island of South Georgia, but this came to an end during the early 2000s.

Left: One of the unofficial patches as worn by crews on 1312 Flight at Mount Pleasant Airfield. (Todd Shugart)

Below: XV201, with drogue trailing, waiting for trade. (Dedicated to the K Crews Collection)

Above: Two Tornado F3s keep XV301 company while patrolling the No Fly Zone around the Falkland Islands. (Dedicated to the K Crews Collection)

Right: The three different types of aircraft that were deployed to RAF Mount Pleasant, Port Stanley: the VC10 tanker, Tornado F3 fighter and Hercules C3. (Dedicated to the K Crews Collection)

Chapter Seven

When RAF Lyneham's last Hercules left the base on 1 July 2011 and climbed away to its new home, a part of what had been normality for the RAF was over: the Hercules and RAF Lyneham had always gone together for the past forty plus years. But while this chapter in the Hercules's life was over, its association with its new base, RAF Brize Norton, was starting a new phase in the aircraft's life! Inside the aircraft's hold were the standards of each of the Hercules squadrons that were relocating: Nos 24, 30, 47 and 70, who were to join Nos 99, 101 and 216 already located at Brize in the joint transportation and airborne refuelling role, flying the C-17, VC10 and Tristar respectively.

A C-130J gets airborne from RAF Brize Norton. (UK MOD, Crown Copyright)

Always a favourite at airshows, XV305 takes pride of place during the celebrations of the type's twenty years in RAF service at RAF Fairford. (Marshall)

A C-130K is glimpsed through the port side engines of a sister while on a training operation. (Chaz Gelder)

RAF Brize Norton is the RAF's largest airfield and a perfect fit for the squadrons flying the Hercules as well as other transport assets. Settling into their new location, operations were quickly up and running, the squadrons fulfilling their flying requirements with no disruption to their operations.

When a fleet relocates to a new airfield the logistics involved in moving all the support infrastructure, personnel and maintenance are immense. This started as early as 2009 when building work started at Brize Norton to accommodate the influx of new aircraft and all that goes with the transfer of four flying squadrons. The total number of aircraft on base rose from twenty-eight to sixty-seven with the arrivals from Lyneham, and by March 2011 over seventy buildings had been refurbished, including Housing, IT, Engineering and everything to do with the infrastructure of the base. The RAF now had a superb base to house all their fixed-wing transport needs, including the new Voyager and Atlas aircraft.

XV214 and XV177 being prepared for the last flight of the C-130K at RAF Brize Norton. (Ian Harding)

Left: Run and break: the last flight of the C-130K above Brize Norton. (Ian Harding)

Below: XV177, the first C-130K to arrive in the UK, was also one of the last flying, as seen on the last day before flying into storage at St Athan. (Chaz Gelder)

The last flight over, all the flight and ground crews pose for the photographers. (Ian Harding)

The end for the Hercules C-130K in RAF service finally came during October 2013, after giving thirty-seven years' service; the final sortie was flown from Brize Norton and this farewell mission was particularly poignant as the first aircraft to arrive way back in 1966 (XV177) was at the forefront of the celebrations. The flight involved both XV177 and XV214 and they flew past various locations that the C-130K had had an association with during its service career. The former airfields of Thorney Island, Lyneham and Filton were all treated to a flypast, as well as current RAF stations, Valley and Lossiemouth to name two. The final ferry flight into storage at St Athan took place the following week – the end to a glorious career for the C-130K.

Brize Norton is also home to the Number 1 Parachute Training School. This links nicely with the transfer of the Hercules fleet as prior to their allocation to Brize, an aircraft had to re-locate from Lyneham to take the Paras airborne for their series of jumps. The main drop zone is just a few miles to the north-east, adjacent to the M40 at Weston-on-the-Green. All of the airborne forces employed by the services, Army, Navy and RAF, are trained at the school in static line jumps up to a maximum height of 12,000 feet.

A C-130J waits for its load of paratroopers while on night exercises. (UK MOD, Crown Copyright)

And jump! How to depart from the tail ramp of a C-130K, by British paratroopers. (Dedicated to the K Crews Collection)

XV200, a Special Forces C-130K, operating feet wet at low level. (Dedicated to the K Crews Collection)

A C-130K performs a flypast against a brilliant sunset. (Dedicated to the K Crews Collection)

Chapter Eight

There are occasions when various different anniversaries are recognised and aircraft are painted up to reflect this, and to celebrate the event. The Hercules has had its fair share of such anniversaries.

Many squadrons have used the large tail as a perfect canvas to exhibit this artwork; at least three aircraft of the Hercules C-130J fleet have in recent years been so adorned.

With its special painted tail showing the 206 Squadron badge, ZH866 is seen at RAF Northolt. (Ian Harding)

A night photo shoot at RAF Northolt with ZH880 and her specially marked tail for 47 Squadron. (Ian Harding)

Celebrating that the RAF has been operating the Hercules for the past fifty years, ZH883 is about to depart from its home base of RAF Brize Norton. (G. Pardoe)

XV206 in its pink livery landing at Nellis Air Force Base, Nevada. (Ian Powell)

ZH880 celebrating 100 years of operations for 47 Squadron with its colourful tail. (D. Ellins)

Celebrating forty years of service with the RAF, XV307 departs RAF Fairford after taking pride of place during the 2006 Royal International Air Tattoo. (K. Wills)

During the late 1980s, two aircraft (XV196 and XV206) were selected for an unusual colour modification – an all-over covering of pink paint. This trial was quite a radical change from the normal camouflage colour that then adorned the Hercules fleet and its selection was to appraise its suitability to assist with operations. The paint was actually applied at Kingsfield Airfield, Cyprus, during June 1988. This was to make the aircraft blend with their surroundings and not be visible from above. Cockpit windows were covered with pink coloured mesh/netting when parked as this stopped any reflections from the sun hitting the windows. Even though the trial only used the Hercules over a short period of time, the colour was used more frequently during the 1991 conflict in the Gulf, where RAF Buccaneers, Tornadoes, Jaguars and a single Tristar were painted pink to aid their camouflage while on active operations.

Another example of additional colour that has been applied to the Hercules in RAF service comes from the age-old tradition of adding nose art to airframes during times of war or conflict. This did happen, although in somewhat limited numbers, when the RAF deployed the aircraft to various operations throughout the world.

Chapter Nine

As with all things, the Hercules C.Mk 1 and C.Mk 3 finally reached the end of their useful life with the RAF and all were withdrawn by the end of October 2013. This was a scheduled process, with various airframes being taken out of service periodically as new C-130J variants were being introduced, firstly to fly with 24 Squadron, then to furnish 30 Squadron. The new aircraft worked side by side with the remaining C-130Ks, which were still operated in the hands of Nos 47 and 70 Squadrons, although 70 did stand down during 2010 to reform during 2014 on the new A400 Atlas transport at RAF Brize Norton.

The C-130Ks that were still active during 1999 were all refurbished examples, although they would be gone before 2014. First to go was XV204, which was withdrawn during August 1998 while at Marshall; this was one of the tanker versions converted for the operation in the Falklands, now no longer required.

The sad sight of what remains of XV294 as she is reduced to a pile of scrap at Marshall of Cambridge. (Chaz Gelder)

Next to go was XV203, which was withdrawn from service on 6 September 2000, though this aircraft found further use and was taken into service with the Sri Lankan Air Force as CR-880, finally SCH-3402, and is still being actively used today.

As the years passed, more aircraft were taken out of service; XV178, XV182, XV189, XV207, XV210, XV215, XV218, XV219 and XV223 were all withdrawn during 2000, some being flown back to Lockheed as part payment for the new C-130Js then being introduced. A couple of aircraft, a C.Mk 3 and C.Mk 1, did get refurbished by Lockheed and are now in service with the Mexican Air Force as 10617 and 10615 respectively.

2001 saw the following aircraft withdrawn during the year: XV176, XV185, XV186, XV187, XV191, XV192, XV195, XV211, XV222, XV297, XV300 and XV306. Once again some aircraft were sent back to Lockheed and further use with the Mexican Air Force, with them taking another C.Mk 1 and C.Mk 3 version.

The year 2002 was a relatively slow year for withdrawals, with only three taking place, XV183, XV190 and XV302; the latter stayed at Marshall for fatigue testing to gain useful information for the rest of the fleet then still in service.

The oldest Hercules was finally scrapped during 2003 at Lockheed's Marietta plant: XV176 was flown back to Georgia following thirty-four years of service. The same year saw XV178 suffer the same fate, also at Lockheed. XV296 was the only other airframe to be withdrawn and was scrapped relatively quickly at Marshall during the year. There were some other withdrawals when XV181 and XV291 were taken out of service with the RAF and entered service with the Austrian Air Force as 8T-CA and 8T-CB respectively.

During 2005 XV184 was stored at Marshall, being joined by XV199 during July 2006 and XV212 during 2009, with XV184 and 199 finally being cut during May 2009. This year also saw the first airframe ending up at Hixon Air & Ground, Staffordshire, when XV197 arrived for storage and eventual scrapping.

December 2008 saw XV294, XV299 and XV307 all arriving for storage at Marshall, all being cut up during February 2012.

Eight of the last of the C-130Ks to be withdrawn from service, XV177, XV188, XV196, XV200, XV209, XV214, XV295 and XV305, were flown direct into storage at the former RAF St Athan in the Vale of Glamorgan, South Wales. These aircraft were maintained in fully airworthy condition for possible onward sale to new customers. The final two to touch down at the base (XV177 and XV214) arrived on 29 October 2013 to join the six already in store within St Athan's mighty super-hangar. Subsequently, two aircraft have flown out to join a private owner (IMP Group in Canada), XV214 taking up the registration C-FNUM when she flew out on 8 December 2015; the other, XV303, took the registration C-FNUL and she departed the UK on 21 November 2015. Both of these aircraft are currently stored in an airworthy condition with their new owner. XV305 also departed St Athan and returned to Lyneham for stripping out and sectioning and was finally transported

Stored C-130K aircraft at Marshall's facility at Cambridge Airport. (Marshall)

Its flying days over, a C-130K sits at St Athan with propeller removed, waiting for its final fate. (Chaz Gelder)

by road to Air & Ground Limited at Hixon Airfield, Staffordshire, during January 2011. This was followed by XV220 and then XV217; these two were withdrawn from service at RAF Lyneham, being stripped and scrapped and finally transported out to Hixon.

Museums have been somewhat reluctant to have any of the C-130Ks in their inventory. This could be down to the sheer size of the aircraft, or it could be that the aircraft doesn't really have the appeal of a fighter or bomber! That said, though, the RAF Museum at RAF Cosford does have one in their collection. XV202, a stretched C3 version, graces the approach to the museum; this aircraft flew into Cosford on 12 August 2011 and is the only C-130K to have been put on display anywhere in the UK. One of the aircraft that was returned to Lockheed, XV183, a C.Mk 3, had also found its way to the Georgetown, Sussex County, airport museum in Delaware; although the aircraft was not in very good condition, the intention was to restore her and display at their facility, but sadly she was in too poor a condition and was scrapped on site during 2016.

XV209 has her outer wings removed while sitting out her days in storage at St Athan's super-hangar. (Chaz Gelder)

Chapter Ten

When Lockheed Martin developed the upgraded version of the Hercules, the J model, they chose the Royal Air Force to be the launch customer. To the uninitiated the new aircraft looks very similar to the traditional C-130K, but the differences soon become apparent. Firstly, the six-bladed composite propellers manufactured by Dowty's in Gloucestershire show that there is a difference with the powerplants: the J versions are powered by four Allison AE 2100D3 turboprops, developing thrust of 4,700 shp each. These propel the aircraft to a maximum speed of 320 knots at an increased height of 40,000 feet. A new digital engine control system

The roll-out of the first J model for the RAF at Lockheed Martin's Marietta manufacturing plant. (Lockheed Martin)

Wearing its American registration N130JA, what would later become ZH865 gets airborne for the first time at Marietta, Georgia. (Lockheed Martin)

gives the aircraft an increased thrust power on take-off and also gives greatly improved fuel efficiency.

The RAF specified a total of twenty-five airframes (ZH865 – ZH889) when the order was placed in December 1994. These were of two variants: C4, similar to but slightly shorter than the C.Mk 3 version, and the C5, which is the same length as the C.Mk 1 variant. The order was split into fifteen aircraft of the C4 version and ten of the C5, these being allocated to Nos 24, 30 and 47 Squadrons initially.

While there were minimal obvious differences on the outside of the aircraft, there were many more on the inside, including a revised glass cockpit that brought the aircraft up to date. This allowed the use of a two-man flight crew, relinquishing the Flight Engineer/Navigator positions, and full Head-Up Displays that permitted all the basic flight data to be transmitted directly in view with the pilot's line of sight, thus allowing complete visual control and full situation awareness. Night vision goggles (NVG) capability is also fully compatible with the aircraft's systems and gives the C-130J an enhanced mission profile over the C-130K, although some of the Special Forces equipped C-130K aircraft did possess a limited compatibility with NVG.

Being able to defend itself is another of the C-130J's strengths; the defensive aids suite includes a missile warning system, and this is linked to a directional infra-red countermeasure system, radar warning receiver and the capability to dispense chaff and flares. The aircraft also has a defensive system to help protect itself against air-to-air and surface-to-air infra-red weapons that the aircraft may come into contact with during operations.

Cambridge Airport and four brand-new C-130Js from Lockheed Martin wait for final checks before entering service. (Marshall)

ZH884, a C5 in overall grey colour with a borrowed green cowling on number 4 engine, while operating through the Welsh countryside. (K Wills)

C-130J ZH879 taxiing in at Marshall Aerospace at Cambridge Airport. This aircraft has the Large Aircraft Infra-Red Countermeasures System (LAIRCM) fitted, as displayed by the turrets containing the lasers, which are visible on the rear of the fuselage, just behind the roundel. (Marshall)

ZH888 showing the portable modular roll on/roll off system that is available for many different applications: medical, VIP, communications, to name a few. (Marshall)

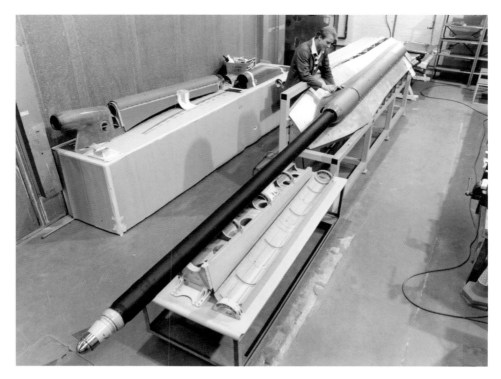

A refuelling probe being prepared prior to installation on a C-130J. (Marshall)

With refuelling probe fitted, an unidentified C-130J waits to enter service at Marshall Aerospace, Cambridge. (Marshall)

Another difference the C-130J has with its predecessor is the location of the in-flight refuelling probe, which is sighted on the left-hand side of the fuselage above the cockpit, the complete opposite of the location on the C-130K version.

Initial deliveries to the RAF commenced during 2000, all being taken into service by the end of 2003. Most of the fleet transited through Marshall, as did the C.Mk 1s prior to their delivery into service; this was to confirm acceptance from Lockheed Martin. The first C-130J (ZH865) was delivered into Boscombe Down Airfield on 26 August 1998 for two years of trials before the fleet could enter operational service. This enabled the flight training programme and manuals to be specified and constructed for all future crew training. ZH865 had also undergone over two years of flight trials in the USA with Lockheed Martin as one of the prototype trials aircraft. Aircraft deliveries were constant during 1998; all were delivered into Cambridge and Marshall and were stored there, fully serviceable, until released to the LTW and RAF service. One aircraft was also flown direct to Lyneham during 1999 when ZH866 arrived on 10 December; this enabled service personnel to get acquainted to their new charge and understand the differences to the old C.Mk 1 variant they knew so well. This also gave the maintenance teams time to examine the requirements and equipment needed to be able to give lineside maintenance to the aircraft; all major maintenance and modification work, though, would still be carried out by Marshall, keeping continuity of all major servicing. Deliveries continued during 1999 and into 2000; the first ten aircraft (ZH865 – ZH874) spent their first year after manufacture flying in the USA, gathering data and information and determining the whole flight envelope before release. One aircraft, ZH868, spent over three years conducting this type of work and was finally delivered to Marshall on 19 October 2000; this was the last aircraft of the fleet to arrive in the UK out of the total of twenty-five, and completed the order to the RAF. ZH875 – ZH889 were delivered within six months of their manufacturing date; the last, ZH889, first flew on 15 May 2000 and was delivered into Marshall just 10 days later on the 25th. To release aircraft so soon after manufacture shows the level of confidence that Lockheed Martin had in the new model as all the flight trials had gathered so much information. The introduction of the C-130J signalled a significant increase in the capabilities of the C-130 fleets in both the Iraq and Afghanistan theatres of operations. The increased capacity of the C-130J allowed the use of a new Container Delivery System (CDS), which permitted the aircraft to carry a maximum of 16 tons of supplies, in 1-ton containers. These loads could be dropped in either one single pass, or on several passes over different drop zones. With improved avionics, the aircraft could release the containers with a higher level of accuracy, even if the drop zone was obscured by cloud or darkness. The CDS was first deployed in July 2006 with excellent results.

The C-130J also performed better than the C-130K during operations in hot and higher altitude conditions and was more reliable. The aging C-130K fleet had been suffering increasingly from serviceability problems, requiring regular rotations back to the UK for maintenance when deployed on operations.

Chapter Eleven

When Saddam Hussain's forces invaded Kuwait on 2 August 1990, it marked a turning point in the region. The United Nations agreed resolution 660 for all Iraqi troops to exit Kuwait immediately. The American Government, under the leadership of George Bush, also gave the Iraqi authorities an ultimatum to leave Kuwait by 15 January 1991 or face the real possibility of war.

XV293, on duty during Operation Granby, lands at a remote airstrip. (Crown Copyright/ Ministry of Defence, Courtesy of Air Historical Branch (RAF))

Always popular during times of conflict, nose art adorned a few of the RAF C-130 fleet during the Gulf War. Here, XV306 *The Baron* sits at RAF Lyneham during a break from service in the Gulf. (K. Wills)

All the warnings fell on deaf ears and during the night of 15/16 January 1991, the American-led coalition forces struck at Iraq and Iraqi troops within Kuwait, a massive airborne military strike that also left the Iraqi Air Force destroyed within a matter of hours of the campaign starting.

This military action could not have taken place until everything was in place within the theatre of operations, primarily Saudi Arabia and the surrounding area. The United States had the lion's share of equipment and hardware, but the UK military forces, the Army, Navy and Royal Air Force, were also there in numbers and the second-largest contingent within the assembled force under the mantle of Operation Granby. All of the support had to be transported from the UK and the Hercules once again proved itself invaluable in this operation.

Lyneham's greatest asset was in very high demand, transporting various supplies in support of Operation Granby; the Hercules fleet brought over 44,642 tons of supplies into the region. The deployment of fighter aircraft was one of the first operational deployments; this was to help police the Northern and Southern 'No Fly Zones' and was crucial in stopping Iraqi forces encroaching on other nations bordering Kuwait. Hercules aircraft rapidly assisted these movements of personnel and equipment to Incirlik in Turkey and Riyadh in Saudi Arabia.

Dennis the Menace, otherwise known as XV292, at Lyneham after hostilities had finished in the Middle East. (K. Wills)

XV190, a stretched C3 version of the C-130K, with artwork on the side door at RAF Lyneham. (K. Wills)

By 9 August 1990, twenty-seven RAF Hercules operated by fifty-seven crews were fully committed to supporting the build-up of British forces, and by 1 November the Hercules force was operating within the Gulf region based out of Riyadh on supply routes, the usual complement being four aircraft at a time employed on these duties. Helicopters forwarded on the supplies to out-stationed troops. RAF Hercules aircraft amassed over 40,000 flight hours and consumed over 24 million gallons of fuel, while flying 12 million miles.

A C-130J being loaded with humanitarian aid for Iraq at RAF Brize Norton. (UK MOD, Crown Copyright)

C-130J ZH869 is guided off the apron at an airfield within Iraq during Operation Telic. (Crown Copyright/ Ministry of Defence, Courtesy of Air Historical Branch (RAF))

A C-130J is loaded with a new Foxhound armoured car at RAF Akrotiri, Cyprus, for onward transportation to Iraq. (Crown Copyright/Ministry of Defence, Courtesy of Air Historical Branch (RAF))

RAF Hercules aircraft remained in theatre once hostilities ended, being utilised for transport operations throughout the region for all Allied forces, as well as operating homeward and into theatre flights for the ongoing requirements needed to maintain a UK presence in the area. During 20 March 2003, Operation Telic was launched to free Iraq of its dictatorial leader and his unwillingness to comply with United Nations Article 1441; twenty-one days of combat operations were underway. This action would lead to the detainment of Saddam Hussein and the end of his reign of power.

All of the four operational Hercules squadrons were active in helping to build-up the forces required for the operation, maintaining an airbridge from the UK via Akrotiri to Kuwait and Fujairah in the United Arab Emirates. From May 2003, sorties began to be flown directly into Basrah International Airport, where a Hercules detachment was established for operations in-country. Operations included moving supplies, equipment and troops around the country, and also conducting aero-medical and repatriation flights; the Hercules also maintained exterior routes to RAF Akrotiri, Al Udeid, Oman and Kuwait. The detachment consisted of two aircraft, but occasionally rose to more for short periods when demand necessitated.

Basrah International Airport did prove to be a hostile environment to operate out of, with regular rocket and mortar attacks against the base and also frequent reports of aircraft coming under small arms, RPG or SAM fire while either landing or taking off. During August 2006 the detachment moved to Al Udeid in Qatar, although aircraft still staged through Basrah on a regular basis. With issues around the Tristar fleet from December 2005, the Hercules took ownership of the airbridge to the UK; at that point the Hercules were conducting all operations for transporting troops on the Qatar–Iraq leg of the route, this being a highly hostile environment with high threat levels for the aircraft and crews to contend with.

C-130Js at Basra. Between 11 November and 12 December 2008, the Hercules detachment implemented the Operation Telic Relief in Place (RiP). Over a six-week period Royal Air Force Hercules C-130Js transported personnel and equipment between Kuwait and Basra, Iraq. (Crown Copyright/Ministry of Defence, Courtesy of Air Historical Branch (RAF))

Above: The C-130J sits on the main ramp at Basra following the Battle of Britain fly-past. (Crown Copyright/Ministry of Defence, Courtesy of Air Historical Branch (RAF))

Right: Basrah Air Station, Iraq, on 15 September 2004 became the dramatic setting for a service to commemorate the Battle of Britain. The guard of honour consisted of twenty personnel drawn from all sections within Basrah Air Station and the parade was also able to include the traditional music and pageantry of a sunset ceremony, complete with fly-past from a locally based C-130 Hercules aircraft. (Crown Copyright/Ministry of Defence, Courtesy of Air Historical Branch (RAF))

Chapter Twelve

RAF Hercules aircraft started to fly sorties between the UK and Oman from October 2001 to support the build-up of forces in Afghanistan under the mantle of Operation Herrick. This route was extended to Kabul in November 2001, with Bagram following in December 2001. All sorties were scheduled to arrive into Kabul at night to aid protection of the aircraft, the crews having to use night vision goggles for their final approaches.

In early 2003 a Hercules detachment was established in Kabul; usually this consisted of one or two aircraft, increasing up to four aircraft when demand required. Crews were provided by the Hercules squadrons on rotation, although there was an amount of operations by mixed crews taking place. Both day and night operations were being flown all around the country, transporting personnel (including senior military or diplomatic figures), equipment and supplies, as well as performing casualty evacuations. Primarily the Hercules detachment only flew inside Afghanistan, although the occasional flight outside the country was also made when required. The regular flights out of the UK to Oman or Kabul were maintained by the UK-based Hercules units and not by the detachment based in theatre.

In 2006 the Hercules detachment moved to Kandahar Airfield, with operations regularly conducted to supply and support isolated garrisons or patrols that were located within Helmand Province. These sorties involved either dropping supplies from low level, or landing on rough temporary airstrips. Without these operations, these detachments would need to be supplied by ground convoys or possibly withdrawn altogether; the dangers to road operations at that time were all too evident.

The wear on the aircraft that were operating in this hot and high environment was considerable, with excessively high rates of wear on the engines and airframes taking their toll. The weather contributed to some exceptional circumstances when five Hercules were damaged by a hailstorm at Kandahar in April 2013.

When British forces started deploying to Afghanistan, the Hercules fleet was once again called upon to get a vast proportion of the equipment into theatre. Under the auspices of Operation Herrick, the Hercules fleet was operated as part of 904 Expeditionary Air Wing (EAW) and is part of RAF headquarters, based at Kandahar Airfield, located close to Afghanistan's second city of Kandahar. This airfield, which is one of the busiest in the world, sees a high proportion of traffic within a twenty-four-hour period.

It is home to a variety of nations who operate a whole remit of different weapons systems and aircraft, including RAF Reaper Remotely Piloted Air Systems (RPAS), helicopters, strategic and tactical lift aircraft such as the RAF Hercules and civilian and contractor aircraft as well as large number of fast jet strike aircraft. These aircraft operate under one umbrella as a single force to provide critical support to the ground forces and contribute to the International Security Assistance Force (ISAF) mission to stabilise and develop Afghanistan within the cultural and humanitarian projects 'Winning Hearts and Minds'.

The C-130J Hercules is used in the tactical support role, being capable of operating from unprepared airstrips and operating in support of ground forces by moving troops and delivering supplies through air drop. Both aircraft types operate extensively in support of British troops, but are also in demand across the entire operating area and will frequently support Coalition forces across the whole of Afghanistan.

C-130K XV177 at rest and waiting for her next mission at Kandahar Airfield during April 2006. (Crown Copyright/Ministry of Defence, Courtesy of Air Historical Branch (RAF))

Another Hercules from the detachment at Kandahar (C-130J ZH879) prepares to leave for a mission under the watchful eye of an air marshaller. (Crown Copyright/Ministry of Defence, Courtesy of Air Historical Branch (RAF))

Two C-130Js, ZH872 and ZH879, in between operations during October 2012 while part of the Hercules detachment during Operation Herrick. (Crown Copyright/ Ministry of Defence, Courtesy of Air Historical Branch (RAF))

ZH877, a C-130J, sits on the apron at Kandahar Airfield, connected to a portable generator and with the back ramp open to try to keep the aircraft cool in the heat of the day. (Crown Copyright/Ministry of Defence, Courtesy of Air Historical Branch (RAF))

With engines running, ground crew at Bastion load up a C-130 with supplies to be delivered in-country during November 2007. (Crown Copyright/Ministry of Defence, Courtesy of Air Historical Branch (RAF))

As darkness falls, C-130J ZH889, the last aircraft produced for the RAF, is prepared for another mission. (Crown Copyright/Ministry of Defence, Courtesy of Air Historical Branch (RAF))

A silhouetted C-130J gets airborne while on Operation Herrick. (UK MOD Crown Copyright)

Three C-130s on the apron at Kandahar Airfield, Helmand Province, Afghanistan. (UK MOD, Crown Copyright)

ZH873, a C-130J, gets airborne from Kandahar Airfield while sister C-130s are sat out on the main apron, waiting for their next mission. Note the lack of refuelling probe above the cockpit. (Crown Copyright/Ministry of Defence, Courtesy of Air Historical Branch (RAF))

The role of the C-130 Hercules in Operation Herrick came to an end on 14 November 2014, when the last two deployed aircraft returned to RAF Brize Norton from Kandahar Airfield, which they departed on the 12th of the month. This marked the end of over twelve years of service for the Hercules force in the Afghanistan arena, aircrew, engineers and a full complement of support personnel ensuring that the mission was attained throughout the aircraft's tenure.

Operation Herrick: a C-130J at Bastion operated by the 904 EAW. (UK MOD, Crown Copyright)

With part of the Hindu Kush mountain range in the distance, a C-130K slows as the back ramp door is already down for an offload, while an RAF Chinook with rotors already running waits to get airborne. (Dedicated to the K Crews Collection)

The view out of the astrodome on the top of the fuselage of a C-130K while operating in the Middle East as part of Operation Herrick. (Dedicated to the K Crews Collection)

A C-130K at rest on Kandahar's apron as the sun goes down. (Dedicated to the K Crews Collection)

The role of the Hercules in theatre was to provide the capability of tactical airlift; this has also proved invaluable in the drawing down of Camp Bastion, with the aircraft transporting huge amounts of freight and stores back to the UK.

Hercules operations in both Iraq and Afghanistan came under the broader campaign codenames of Operation Telic (Iraq) and Operation Herrick (Afghanistan). While some particular sorties, especially in-country, may have been made under other specific sub-operations, the vast majority came under the broader heading.

There were still operational requirements under the mantle of Operation Herrick as personnel were deployed until the end of 2014; the operation then changed to Operation Toral, the British commitment to NATO's support mission, even though there were no personnel on active duty from the Air Mobility force.

904 EAW patch, as worn by some aircrew and the 904 HQ personnel during Operation Herrick. (Todd Shugart)

The amount of dust that the C-130s kicked up during operations from desert strips is apparent in this view of one landing in a remote location. (Dedicated to the K Crews Collection)

XV196 photographed through night vision goggles (NVGs) at Bastion. (Dedicated to the K Crews Collection)

A C-130K comes to a halt and demonstrates its rough landing capabilities. (Dedicated to the K Crews Collection)

Chapter Thirteen

In the event of hostilities, the RAF Hercules fleet would initially come under national (Government) control before being assigned to NATO command. With NATO designating the deployment of British forces, the Hercules would then transport, resupply and reinforce with arms and equipment, return flights being used to evacuate any wounded personnel. Additionally the Hercules could be assigned by the UK Government to evacuate any British nationals deemed to be in imminent danger. This may also utilize other forces to secure a section of strategic territory and possibly supply reinforcements using air-landed troops to make any such operations successful. To support these operations, Hercules crews train on a regular basis with Britain's intervention force, Number 5 Airborne Brigade, which forms a part of NATO's Joint Rapid Deployment Force (JDF).

ZH870, a C-130J C4, and an unidentified sister taxiing at RAF Brize Norton. Note the lack of refuelling probe above the cockpit area.

A view inside the cockpit on a C-130K at low level through the Welsh countryside, showing the level of concentration exhibited by the crew. (Chaz Gelder)

ZH865 training on Salisbury Plain. (Ian Harding)

There were a few C-130Ks that appeared somewhat different from the main fleet; these are the Special Forces (SF) equipped machines. Painted in an all-over green livery with various lumps and bumps scabbed on the fuselage and under the wings, the actual specification of these aircraft remains somewhat classified to this day. Operated by 47 Squadron, the aircraft could carry four heavily armed Special Forces Land Rovers and land-based and water-based troops who could parachute from the aircraft at medium and high altitudes. RAF SF Hercules were equipped with a defensive aids sub-system (DASS), designed to detect and protect against SAMs (surface-to-air missiles). The DASS consists of AN/AAQ-24(V) Nemesis directed IR countermeasures (DIRCM), an AN/AAR-47 electro-optical missile warning system and AN/APR-39A Radar Warning Receivers, generically known as Skyguardian, as well as three AN/ALE-40 chaff/flare dispensers on either side of the lower nose.

In addition to the defensive avionics, SF Hercules were also fitted with a suite of sensor systems as part of an Enhanced Vision System upgrade: a SIGMA Thermal Imaging system (in a Titan 385 turret under the aircraft's nose) and a Low Light

A demonstration of how quickly troops can be deployed from a C-130K during an air display. (Dedicated to the K Crews Collection)

XV291 de-icing prior to a mission underneath a dramatic sky. (Dedicated to the K Crews Collection)

Level Television (LLLTV) camera (in a fixed array above the nose) These sensor packages allowed the SF Hercules to better operate at night and in poor weather conditions.

RAF SF Hercules could also accommodate an array of classified listening gear, which allows 47 Squadron to fly SIGINT (SIGnals INTelligence) missions.

Other advanced avionics found in SF flight Hercules included: a Honeywell 764G GPS/INS navigation system, a QinetiQ W advanced mission computer, Flat Panel avionics displays and a Goodrich Sensor Systems digital air data computer. As an aid to flight crews, flight deck armour was later added to protect the crew from ground fire in hostile situations.

Two Special Forces equipped C-130Ks flying at low level over the California countryside while operating out of Naval Air Weapons Station China Lake. (Dedicated to the K Crews Collection)

A Special Forces C-130K training on Pembrey Sands during July 2005.

Chapter Fourteen

Unfortunately, whenever you have a large fleet of aircraft there is always the possibility of aircraft losses via training or on operational missions. The Hercules suffered from quite a low percentage of such accidents, with around 250,000 flying hours per incident. XV180 was the first to be written off when, on 24 March 1969, the aircraft was taking off from RAF Fairford and the captain asked the co-pilot to feather number 4 engine; the engine, though, went into full reverse and caused the aircraft into an uncontrollable starboard wing over. The aircraft crashed and caught fire, with the loss of all the crew on board.

The next loss for the RAF came on 9 November 1971, when XV216 from 24 Squadron crashed into the sea off Pisa in Italy. This was with the loss of forty-six Italian paratroopers as well as all of the crew of the aircraft.

The remains of XV198 after she crashed into the woods north-east of Colerne Airfield on 10 September 1973. (© Bath in Time)

A bench memorial, in the church grounds at South Cerney, to the crew of XV180, which crashed at RAF Fairford in 1969. (C. Bennett)

XV194 was the third C.Mk 1 to crash when it veered off the runway while landing at Tromsø Airport, Norway, on 12 September 1972; the aircraft ended up in a ditch. There were no fatalities but the aircraft was damaged beyond repair.

Nearly exactly one year later, on 10 September 1973, XV198 from 48 Squadron crashed at RAF Colerne, Wiltshire. Performing training for the co-pilot, the aircraft overshot from runway 07 with a simulated engine out failure when the remaining engine on the same side failed. With the aircraft at a height of only 400 feet and at a low airspeed, the aircraft suffered from asymmetrical power from the two working engines, which made the aircraft totally uncontrollable. XV198 impacted the ground with the loss of all five on board.

It was over ten years until the next incident affected the Hercules fleet. On 27 June 1985 XV206 collided with a Royal Navy Sea King Helicopter HAS 5 (XZ919) from 826 Naval Air Squadron, at a height of about 200–300 feet in cloud just to the north of the Falkland Islands. The Hercules lost most of its wing outboard of number 1 engine but the Sea King was lost along with its crew; XV206 managed to land safely and was repaired and put back into service.

1993 brought the next loss, this time XV193 when it crashed at Glen Loch, Blair Atholl, Perthshire, stalling after a cargo drop. All on board were killed: eight RAF crew and one member from the Army.

XV298 was written off on 11 January 1999, when she crashed on take-off from Kukes airstrip, Albania, when it hit an obstacle and caught fire; there were no fatalities.

30 January 2005 was a very sad day indeed for the Hercules and the RAF. XV179 crashed after it was hit by insurgent fire while routing from Baghdad to Balad, Iraq. This started a fire in the starboard wing tank, which caused an explosion that sealed the aircraft's fate: all ten crew members were sadly killed.

XV206 had its second incident during 24 May 2006 while flying for 47 Squadron on a Special Forces flight. The new British Ambassador was also on board when it crash landed outside Lashkar Gar, Helmand Province, on a dirt landing strip. The aircraft hit a landmine, which caused a fire in the aircraft's port external fuel tank and set number 2 engine on fire. Nine crew and twenty-six passengers all exited the aircraft safely and she was left to burn; it was later revealed that the majority of the passengers were SAS troops and that there was a large amount of money on board that was allegedly destined for local warlords for their intelligence in the ongoing war against the Taliban.

The first of the new C-130J C4 variant had an incident on 12 February 2007 when ZH876 was seriously damaged while landing in Maysan Province in Iraq, close to the Iranian border.

Even though the aircraft was relatively new, the risk for Coalition forces to recover the aircraft was too high so orders were given to destroy the aircraft in situ. The aircraft was also carrying secure communications equipment, which could not be allowed to fall into the wrong hands and compromise future missions. This was the first loss of the new C-130J for any nation flying this version since their introduction in 1999.

XV205 landed heavily during 23 August 2007 at an airstrip in Afghanistan, deep in the heart of Taliban-controlled territory. Operated by a Special Forces flight crew from 47 Squadron, the aircraft was badly damaged and, like ZH876, could not be safely recovered so it was destroyed in place by British troops to protect the equipment and capability of the Special Forces aircraft. There were no reports of any casualties.

The last recorded incident for the Hercules occurred on 6 May 2010 when XV304 landed at Brize Norton on its belly due to an issue with its undercarriage. Because of the need for spare parts to keep the remaining C.1 versions airworthy, the decision was made not to repair XV304 and to use all wing panels for the aircraft undergoing overhaul at Marshall. The fuselage of XV304 still exists in the hands of the Joint Air Delivery Test and Evaluation Unit (JADTEU) at RAF Brize Norton as a training aid.

Out of the ninety-one aircraft that have been operated by the Royal Air Force, a total of eleven have been written off over the past forty-one years. Since 2005 all the major losses have occurred within areas of conflict, and then only one of these involved the loss of life. While this is no comfort to the families of the crew, it does show that the Hercules is one of the safest types within the inventory. Its ability to withstand damage and still get its passengers and crews safely back to terra firma is testament to the aircraft's design.

Chapter Fifteen

Currently there are twenty-one Hercules C-130J models in service with the RAF, one having been written off during operations and three in storage at Marshall of Cambridge, all fully airworthy. The arrival of the A400 Atlas into service has impacted the need for the Hercules, but the requirements for this tactical airlifter still remain.

The wing centre replacement programme that was announced by the British Government during July 2017 will see Marshall Aerospace contracted to carry out this work on fourteen of the RAF's C-130J C4 aircraft. The installation of these Centre Wing Box Kits will enhance the service life of the wing, increasing the life by two to three times more than the original fitted when the aircraft were new. Lockheed Martin will manufacture the kits and they will be installed at the Marshall Aerospace facility at Cambridge. This will enable the Hercules to carry on serving the RAF and to still be seen in the skies over the UK.

A C-130J in the circuit at RAF Brize Norton at sunset. (D. Ellins)

ZH889 on a training flight through LFA 7, the low fly area in Wales. (D. Ellins)

16 Air Assault Brigade jump from a C-130J Hercules aircraft over Salisbury Plain, Wiltshire, during Exercise Wessex Storm. (UK MOD, Crown Copyright)

A C-130J landing at Brize Norton as dusk falls. (Ian Harding)

Acknowledgements

With thanks to A. Paul, Marshall Aerospace; Stephanie Stinn, Lockheed Martin; W. Ragg; Lee Barton, Air Historical Branch (RAF); P. Wise, K Crew Collections; and many others for supplying various images. A very special thank you is extended to Lt-Col. Todd Shugart, USAF